Social Media Made Simple

Social Media Marketing Tips for Small Business:
A Quick Guide to Boosting your Brand with 101 Free Content Ideas

The Sitters Australia

Contact:

sian@thecloudsitters.com.au

Table of Contents

About This Book

One of the best ways to establish the personality behind your business is through social media marketing. Social media platforms, essentially, act as a channel to showcase the "voice" of your business with educational and (hopefully, fun!) content. Plus, they drive traffic to your website.

But we don't need to tell you how important it is to have a social media presence. If you're a small business owner, you've probably seen numerous ads from marketing agencies on your newsfeed, sprouting lines like "if you're not on social media, you're invisible". So why aren't more business owners working furiously on their marketing plans?

Because, who's got time for that? In small business, we can all appreciate that time = money!

This is one of the main complications we see preventing small business owners from plunging into the social media space and building their brands online. The next biggest hurdle? Not knowing where to start.

We have designed this book to be YOUR starting point. Each section contains bite-sized pieces of knowledge to tear down the "overwhelm" and get your social media happening – as painlessly as possible - in five quick steps:

1. **Research** (it sounds boring, but skipping this step is like making an omelette without eggs. No foundation! We'll make it quick; we promise.)

2. **Setting up your accounts** to showcase the best features of your brand.

3. **Scheduling content** that is engaging, drives traffic and produces leads.

4. **Evaluating** along the way to make sure what you're doing is working.

5. Using your evaluations to **implement a social media strategy** that provides results for your business (without taking up too much of your valuable time!)

We have jam-packed our book with case studies, examples and mini tasks so you can dive in and get your marketing done and dusted straight away! Your pace is up to you.

Take the time to complete the tasks for each chapter before moving on to the next one. By the end, you will have your own customised social media marketing plan ready to go, whether you decide to implement it yourself or outsource.

Tip: Before we get started, find yourself some writing paper or a notebook!

This book is designed for business owners with limited marketing experience; those who may have dipped a toe into the social media pond, but who essentially are "winging it" and hoping for the best.

It can be experienced in two ways:

1. A chronological process. If you are completely new to marketing, we recommend reading this book through from start to finish. Take an afternoon off, sit down and work through the activities step by step to start preparing your business for online growth.

2. The answer to your burning questions. If your business is at a more advanced stage in its marketing journey, you can feel free to jump straight ahead to the chapter you need.

If you have any questions about the content in this book, or need clarification on where to find certain features within your social media accounts, please don't hesitate to send an email to our marketing team:

sian@thecloudsitters.com.au

We are more than happy to help answer any questions you might have (free of charge, of course!)

Step 1: A Little Bit of Research

"The harder you work for something, the greater you'll feel when you achieve it."
Unknown

Your Audience is Not Everybody.

First thing's first. Your audience is not everybody.

If you were scrolling through your newsfeed and spotted an ad for dog collars (even though you don't have any pets), would you click on it?

Maybe. You might be seeking a gift for your sister's dog. But most likely, it's not going to be relevant to you, and the dog collar company has unfortunately wasted a valuable little slice of their marketing budget.

Here's another example. You're a small business selling cupcakes. As delicious as cupcakes are, we can't assume that everybody loves them as much as we do! Every dollar counts when it comes to marketing, so it's essential to make sure your advertising is delivered only to the newsfeeds of cupcake enthusiasts.

Luckily, we don't need to go searching for a needle in a haystack. Today's technology allows us to reach an amazing array of demographics – right down to spending habits, careers and interests!

So, who is your audience?

Tip: Your current and previous customers are a great starting point to answering this question.

Mini Task

Make a list of your current and previous clients. You might have access to software that can generate this report for you, but here are a few basic factors to identify first:

CONSTRUCTION INDUSTRY
? MAINTENANCE

- ➢ Age Group

- ➢ Occupation

- ➢ Family Status

- ➢ How they heard about you. If you aren't doing this already, make it a habit to ask this question each time you receive a new customer or prospect.

Are you starting to see a pattern? You might notice that your customers are mostly Generation Y stay-home mums who found you on Facebook. This information is GOLD because it tells you who you should tailor your message to, and what platform to run your advertising on.

If you are in your early stages of business without an established client list, have a think about what customers you would choose if you had the option. For example, if you own a small printing company and you have an extensive background working in retail, you might start off by targeting retailers. You probably already know a great deal about the types of promotional items and signage they typically use, so you're in a great position to send your communications in that direction.

Another option is to leverage the insights you already have on your social media business profiles (if available).

Mini Task

Browse the "Insights" section of your Facebook, Instagram, or LinkedIn accounts to find out more about your followers; for example, their age, occupation, and what time of day they use social media. Write this information down in your notebook.

Remember: you can contact us at any time if you are not sure where to find your insights. Our contact information can be found at the beginning of this book.

Personas

Now that we have a broad customer outline, we can break this down even further into a persona – an actual profile for your <u>perfect</u> customer.

You might be thinking, "I'm only just starting my business, I'm not going to turn people away just because they don't fit my persona!"

And we would agree with you. If you are at the stage of your business where you can be selective about which clients you take on, the persona is perfect for ensuring you reach the right people (and even more handy if you have staff to train).

If you own a products-based business or are a newbie in the small business world, the persona is handy to keep in mind because it will provide marketing direction. Of course, we don't encourage turning down business, but determining the customer type you aspire to serve will bring clarity to your marketing journey.

So, let's draw that customer of yours!

Mini Task

1. Give your customer a name. Is he a David, a Luke – maybe a Karen?

2. Where does Karen live?

3. What age range does she fall into?

4. What does she do for a job?

5. What are Karen's interests? What Facebook / Instagram pages does she follow?

6. What are Karen's pain points (in relation to your product or service?)

7. What does Karen want, essentially?

8. How much would she be willing to spend?

9. Where would she go looking for a product or service she needs?

10. What products does she buy?

11. What factors are important to her? (e.g. price, customer service, results, etc.)

12. Last (but not least!), draw your customer.

Don't worry, we are no artists! But a rough sketch or even a Google Search online will provide you with the photo and the vision for your customer. Get a little creative! Pin it up on the wall to be seen by your team. It might seem silly, but this visual cue will be an extremely valuable reminder of who is reading your social media content.

Is Karen interested in what you're posting? Are you providing Karen with value?

See below a simple example of a persona we have drawn for a personal trainer. Karen's "sweet spots" are written in cursive; her pain points are written in typewriter font.

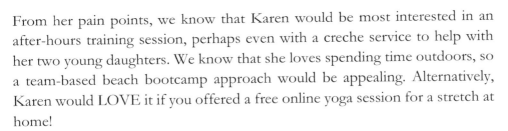

Spends most weekends at the beach

Works in Professional Services

Enjoys the social aspects of team fitness training

2 daughters aged 3 and 6

CONCERNED ABOUT HER PHYSICAL HEALTH AS SHE FEELS SHE HAS LIMITED TIME FOR EXERCISE

Will search on Google for a product or service, and pays particular attention to reviews!

CONSIDERS HERSELF TO BE EXTREMELY TIME POOR

Karen

35-40 years old

HUSBAND WORKS AN ALTERNATE SCHEDULE TO HER OWN

Lives on the Sunshine Coast

Loves to spend time outdoors with her family

LIMITED MOVEMENT DURING THE DAY AS SHE WORKS A DESK JOB

Fitness Budget: $60 / week

Enjoys yoga and would like to invest more in self care

Hopes to wear a nice slimming dress to her cousin's wedding

From her pain points, we know that Karen would be most interested in an after-hours training session, perhaps even with a creche service to help with her two young daughters. We know that she loves spending time outdoors, so a team-based beach bootcamp approach would be appealing. Alternatively, Karen would LOVE it if you offered a free online yoga session for a stretch at home!

You also need to be aware of Karen's possible objections, so that you can tailor your messaging to overcome this before she has a chance to even think of it herself.

For example, one of Karen's objections might be: "I'm too old for personal training, I will probably injure myself."

In this case, your messaging on social media might sound something like this:

Build your strength gently and efficiently with our supportive and qualified personal trainers. We work with your pace to achieve the results you desire.

Now you should have: a complete list of the things that are important to Karen, a summary of her possible objections and hopefully, a wonderful portrait to match!

Note: Don't lose this list under the paperwork in your office and forget all about it. Keep it close and refer to it when scheduling your social media content. Redraw it occasionally, if you need to.

Simply gaining an awareness of Karen's problems and interests will help you to tailor your content in a more personalised and genuine manner, all increasing your chances of generating revenue from the people that need your product or service most.

The best bit? You haven't even spent a cent on marketing yet!

Tip: If you are not sure what your Karen looks like, start with one of your customers as an example. Avoid basing your persona entirely on this person but pick out the elements that best embody your target audience (or your preferred target audience).

Niches

A quick note on niches. While you were drawing up your customers earlier, you might have uncovered a specific segment of customers ideal to your business.

Focusing on a niche market is not compulsory, but it can be profitable to your overall business strategy, because it allows you to position yourself as the "go-to" brand for a particular audience.

Here's an example. You own an accounting firm. You manage the financials for many dental professionals in your local area. Therefore, your customer's name is Ben – he is a dentist.

Instead of competing with the six other accountants in your local area, you might market your services to dentists instead:

"Accounting Experts for Dental Professionals"

How impressive does that sound? All of a sudden, you are an "expert!"

Without knowing anything else about you, one can already assume that you are strongly familiar with the billing systems for dentists, taxes, industry regulations, insurances, etc.

If I were a dentist in the area, I know who I would contact first.

Note: Marketing to a niche is optional. It also does not mean you can't provide accounting services to other business types that approach you. Of course not! But you'll find that your spend and effort will be greatly reduced by marketing to one group only – and doing it well.

Gone are the days of trying to be "everything to everybody!"

Are you a Good Listener?

True or false: The first step of marketing is to become a storyteller.

False! Listening is in fact, the preferred first step of marketing. Listening to the market itself, listening to the competition, but most of all, listening to your customer.

(*Note:* Storytelling is still important! We'll get to this later).

This notion is actually one of the most deceiving things about marketing. People think it's all about communicating to customers; sending out lots of content, delivering messages, talking all the time. But just like any other relationship, this one is a two-way street. So, it's time to become a better listener!

A common mistake that business owners make (often without realising) is to create social media content that appeals to them, assuming of course, that it appeals to everybody.

Unless you identified yourself as your ideal customer earlier in the book, this could not be further from the truth. Even if you love reading your own content, this unfortunately does not mean it is valuable to the people who really need to see it (the persona you drew earlier). If only!

9

That's why it pays to LISTEN before typing out novels. It would be a real shame to spend all that time and effort on a winning story, for nobody to read and enjoy it.

So, next step: find out what it is that your customers really want to read about.

Mini Task

Take note of the following as you scroll your newsfeeds or browse online:

> ➢ Are there any customer trends or content that has gone viral?
>
> ➢ What are you competitors doing?
>
> ➢ What are your customers saying?
>
> ➢ What are they complaining about?
>
> ➢ What are they loving?
>
> ➢ Where is there confusion – can you help to answer any questions?

You don't need to spend endless hours on this. Simply having a basic awareness of your surroundings will give you an edge when it comes to content creation.

Remember this: an engaged audience will spend longer reading your content, click on more ads, and essentially buy more products. Winning!

Optional Mini Task

This exercise focuses on your own business services as opposed to the industry overall. It will be well worth the effort if you are able to make the time.

Chat to your current clients about your services (perhaps just a few of your best and longest standing). If you are a products business, do you have any repeat customers you can contact?

Your conversation can be a quick phone call, an email survey, a general email, or our personal favourite is to enjoy a morning out of the office and set up a meeting over coffee.

Think about how you might ask the following questions:

- ➢ Are you satisfied with the level of service we provide?

- ➢ How can we improve?

- ➢ Is there any area of our services you're unsure about?

- ➢ What type of social content would you like to see more of? What would be most helpful?

- ➢ Do you have any suggestions?

In some cases, it might not be easy to listen to criticisms. But rather than looking for sugar-coated responses, you will find the most value in the feedback that is genuine and honest.

Happy listening!

Step 2: Setting Up for Success

"Action is the foundational key to all success."
Pablo Picasso

Which Platforms will you Choose?

The content you share will always depend on the platform you are posting on (unfortunately "one size fits all" does not work on social).

Have a think about what profiles you'd like to use to showcase your product or service – noting that this will vary from business to business.

If you have a big database of business associates, blogs and professional articles to share, LinkedIn might be your platform of choice. If you have more social connections and a willingness to experiment with images and hashtags, you might choose Facebook or Instagram.

Whatever you choose, it's important to include on your profiles as much information about your business as possible. The reason for this is twofold: to let customers know exactly what they can expect if they engage in your services, but also to increase your searchability (i.e., the likelihood a customer might find your account when searching for a local hairdresser, for example).

This brings us to our next point.

Keywords

Think about what a customer might search for if they need a hairdresser. What would you type into Google? Here are some examples:

Best Hairdresser Brisbane
Cheap Hairdresser Near Me
Hairdressing Services Brisbane
Half Head Foils Brisbane

Next, we pick out the keywords in these search phrases. They might be words like **Hairdresser**, **Foils** or **Brisbane**.

It's important to conduct this research first, so that you can use these words when you create your social media accounts. Having the right keywords will significantly increase your searchability, so take the time now to find out what yours are.

Mini Task

Write down 5 different phrases you think people might use to search for your product or service on Google.

From those 5 phrases, pick out your keywords and write them down. Remember, you will be using these when it comes to writing up your profile information.

Note: It is super important to incorporate keywords into your digital marketing efforts. Does this mean you should throw them wherever you possibly can into all of your text?

Absolutely not. This is referred to as "keyword stuffing" and in some cases, you can be penalised for doing this.

Here is an example of what NOT to do:

Your Brisbane Hairdresser's Hairdressing Services – Hairdressers experienced at Hair and Hairdressing for all your Hairdressing and Hair Needs.

Why might you get penalised for this? Well, put simply: it is absolutely hideous to read. Nowadays, people can see right through your keyword stuffing tactics and will not stick around to read your 50th repetition of the word "hair".

13

Your readers don't like it – your social media doesn't like it – your profile won't like it.

Profile Photo

Your chosen profile picture will depend on the platform/s you've chosen. For example, on Facebook and Instagram, we simply recommend using your business logo. Remember though that the logo is currently in a circle format, so make sure it can be cropped to fit within the edges.

If it doesn't fit neatly, consider taking a snippet of your logo and using this to identify yourself on social media. You can see an example of how we have achieved this for The CloudSitters below:

Complete Logo

The CloudSitters ™
A U S T R A L I A

Social Media Icon

If you are on LinkedIn however, you should use a photo of yourself. Your profile picture is one of the first things that people see. A high-resolution portrait photo, preferably of a professional nature, simply makes you look more human (and therefore, more trustworthy!)

Bio Section (Short & Sweet)

When people read your Instagram bio, they are probably not reading it at all. They might only look for a second or two (we are impatient beings in today's digital world!)

That means you'll need to communicate exactly what it is you do - really quickly. Our advice? Use dot points and if it suits the style of your business, emojis.

For example, if you want to communicate that your products are eco-friendly, you might create a singular dot point with the eco-friendly emoji beside it. Because this is a visual cue, your audience will instantly get the message without having to read any text:

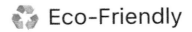

Here's a bio example from Instagram:

The first line **"Small Business Bookkeeping"** is where your "Name" is entered. However, instead of entering your business name, we recommend entering your keywords. If somebody is searching for a bookkeeper on

Instagram, they are likely to enter "Small Business Bookkeeping" or something similar, which is why we have used this phrase instead of **"The BookSitters"**.

Remember, if people haven't heard of your business yet, they certainly won't be searching for it by name! Don't worry, we'll use the business name later on in the text.

The next line has been used the highlight the business slogan, communicating who The BookSitters are in a nutshell: **"Painting the Picture Behind Your Numbers"**.

The following three dot points showcase the key features of the business; its name, where the bookkeepers are located, plus access to a free training course which serves as a lead capture tool for the company. At a glance, we don't know everything there is to know about this business. But we know the important things!

Don't forget about the keywords you wrote down earlier. Here's another example. If you are a dog walker on the Gold Coast, your dot points might read something like this:

➢ Professional Dog Walking Services

➢ Gold Coast Based

➢ Specialising in Large Breeds

➢ We just ADORE dogs!

From these simple points, we know these people love dogs, we know where their services are offered, and we know whether or not they will take our giant Great Dane for a walk. Perfect!

Mini Task

Write your own Instagram Bio using the keywords you identified earlier. If you don't yet have an Instagram account, you can start off by writing your dot points in your trusty marketing notebook.

Tip: If you are having trouble creating a new line within the Instagram app, write your dot points in a "Notes" app first and copy/paste from there.

About Section (Telling a Tale)

Even though technology is evolving to create a more customised experience for users, the process of making a purchase online can still feel very impersonal, especially if you are a service provider and never get to meet your customers.

This is why the "About" section of your profile – whether it is your website, Facebook or LinkedIn page – is your opportunity to showcase the face behind your business.

Think of this page as a summary of all the things that make your business what it is. Below are some examples of topics you might choose to cover:

➢ Tell us about your products or services (most businesses focus solely on this point, but you stand a much better chance of standing out if you pick a few other unique talking points – see below)

➢ What year was your business founded?

➢ Tell us how your business began. People love to read stories of humble beginnings as they serve as inspiration!

➢ How was it founded? What problem were you trying to solve in the marketplace?

➢ Tell us about you (or the owner/founder of the business)

➢ Milestones? (e.g. your first employee, your first sale)

➢ Tell us the best thing about your business and why customers should choose you over your competition?

➢ Can you reveal what clients tell you about your business?

17

➢ Do you have any case studies to share? For example, ways you have helped your clients to grow their business or shine at an event?

➢ What are some of your greatest achievements? (Be careful not to sound boastful here. Consider selecting just a couple of your best achievements that are directly related to your business. For example, as a bookkeeper you might include "Xero Gold Partner").

Not sure which ones to pick? Why not cover them all? By answering each of the points above you are simultaneously telling your story, establishing a human connection while educating customers about your products, services and how they may benefit from them.

The best "About" pages document the history of your brand from a personal perspective. If this page is constantly in a state of "work in progress" - that's okay! Your story will change as your business grows, just don't forget to bring your audience along for the journey.

If creative writing is not your strong point, you can answer these questions in your own words (dot points, if you prefer), then outsource the task to an expert. There are some amazing writers available with very reasonable hourly rates.

The Feed vs The Story

We are often asked to explain the difference between your feed and your stories on Instagram, including when it is appropriate to use each of these.

The feed is essentially your "gallery". See below for what we mean by this:

This gallery is using a balanced blend of content to visually demonstrate what their business is all about at a simple glance:

- ➤ Photos of the team allow the audience to make a human connection with the brand.

- ➤ Inspirational quotes give viewers an insight into the attitudes and values of the business.

- ➤ Use of Xero "Gold Partner" logos showcase their alliance with a global industry leader.

- ➤ Photos of the office give the viewer a "behind the scenes" preview.

- ➤ Testimonials showcase strong customer relationships.

When somebody visits your profile, this page is what they will see first, so you must make sure it only contains content that really makes your brand shine.

For example, if you are a builder and you'd like to showcase a Before/After scenario, we recommend using your "After" photo first so that all of your stunning finished works are available to view when anybody visits your profile. In the text, you might write something like this:

This stunning bathroom has had a complete makeover! We chose neutral colours to create a fresh, modern feel and our client is in love with the final result. Swipe to see what we started with!

The Instagram story is more often used for timely occasions – for example, videos of an event you hosted or behind the scenes snippets of your office shenanigans. You can still showcase your story videos in a highlight reel, but the feed is the first visual point and should be saved for all your best (and prettiest) content.

Put simply, save the best bits for your feed! Post anything else (especially videos) on your stories.

Hashtags

If you haven't already, you will probably hear a lot of conflicting talk about hashtags; whether or not to use them, whether they work, how many to use, etc.

In our experience, *use them!*

Hashtags are a free pathway to getting your content seen by the right people. Why wouldn't you take advantage of this? Especially if you don't intend to invest in paid ads.

So, where do we start? Your keywords. Let's use the example of a locksmith.

1. Select a branded hashtag. This will allow you to collect your content under the one term, for example, we might use a business name like #TheGreatestLocksmith.

2. Next, let's pick some industry-related hashtags. Think #SecuritySolutions #Locksmithing #Locksmith

3. And now, some hashtags that relate to the post or image itself, for example #CarKeys #CutKeys #Safe #BehindTheScenes #LockedOut

Note: Different platforms allow and prefer different quantities of hashtags (e.g., Instagram in 2021 allows a maximum of 30 hashtags). Conduct a little research to find out what best practice is.

Tip: It's important to avoid using hashtags with low popularity.

There's no point using a hashtag if nobody is searching for it! A good way to gage this is to type your hashtag (e.g. #Locksmith) into the search bar. Since it returns about 277,000 results, it's a relatively safe bet. But if we were to try #LocksmithTips with only 200 results, we might consider something different. Use the generated suggestions to get creative with your tags!

Tip: Keep a consistent selection for most posts (e.g., your branded hashtag and your industry keywords), then mix up the remaining hashtags, depending on the post content.

This will allow you to reach different audiences each time. Copying and pasting your consistent hashtags will save lots of time – but remember to monitor their performance and change them where necessary.

Which brings us to our next point. How do you know if you are using the right hashtags?

Let's take Instagram as an example. Have a look at your latest post. Click **"View Insights"** and scroll to the **"Discovery"** section where you can see where your viewers came from. Did they find you via your hashtags?

Have a look below for an example:

1,271

Accounts reached
85% weren't following

Follows	1
Reach	1,271
Impressions	1,326
From hashtags	1,041
From home	182
From profile	100
From other	3

We can see that from the 1,326 views of this post, 1,041 of them came from a hashtag search. That's about **82%**! So, we can give ourselves a pat on the back knowing that we've chosen some fantastic hashtags. Moving forward, we might use the same hashtags again, but mix them up a little to match the content of the new post.

Remember to keep an eye on these insights as they will likely change as trends do!

Mini Task

Write down your top 10-20 hashtags using a blend of branded and industry related. You can copy and paste some of these when you start scheduling your posts!

Scheduling

Later in the book we are going to throw you a whole bunch of social media content ideas (if you haven't been impatient and had a sneak peek already!).

If you haven't already got one, it's time for you to find a social media scheduling tool.

With the right software, you can schedule a whole month's worth of social media posts (or more) in one go. Phew!

But here's a plot twist: scheduling tools can actually do a lot more than just schedule!

Some come with approval systems (fantastic if you are working in a team, with clients or with virtual assistants); others with amazing metrics tools (more on this later), and some will even provide you with hashtag suggestions.

Most offer a free trial period so that you can experiment a little first, so try out a few different platforms to see which you like best! If you don't need all the fancy stuff and are only using a couple of social profiles, you might pick one with a free plan.

Every business is different, so we encourage you to take a bit of time now to find yourself an amazing tool that is going to work well for your business.

Mini Task

Find and sign up for an amazing scheduling tool!

When business owners are under the pump, marketing unfortunately is one of the first things to get cut from the diary. But here is something important to remember:

"Successful firms never stop marketing."
Peter Drucker

Pencil a little bit of marketing time into your schedule each week and ditch the "I'll get to it when I get to it" approach. That way, when business owners are ready to make the switch or invest in your services, you will already be right in front of them.

Step 3: Launching into Content

"Procrastination is opportunity's natural assassin."
Victor Kiam

There's a Reason it's called "Social" Media

This might be one of our most important lessons, and if you happen to follow us on Instagram (**@thecloudsitters**), you've probably heard us run on about it a thousand times.

It is NOT called "Sales" media. Do not use social media to bombard people with sales messages. Nobody wants to follow that. Maybe on occasion – but rarely.

Imagine this. You have just walked in to your first networking meeting. You can see there's a group of 10-15 other people there, presumably all from different industries. You've just grabbed a coffee and a young lady with a laptop and a warm smile is approaching you. What do you say?

Option A: Hi there! Did you know we offer three marketing packages to suit different business owners? We also offer a free consultation to begin with and we accept a variety of different payment options. Get started today! Here is my business card, I hope you will give me a call!

Option B: Hi there! I'm Meg – great to meet you. What brings you to the networking group?

Obviously, the conversation may not be as forward as this, but you can see the point. In everyday life, you would never engulf someone with sales messages as soon as you met them. Even in a networking group – where the entire point of the gathering is to generate leads — friendly banter is always preferable to the hard sell, especially if you're meeting these people for the first time.

The social media world should be no different. It's all about being "social"; allowing your potential customers to get to know the face behind your business. At the end of the day, people connect with PEOPLE, not businesses.

Show them you are not just here to make a sale! Your following will thank you for it.

What's your POD?

The advertising noise around us today is LOUD. It is so deafening that most of the time, we don't even realise we are being exposed to marketing messages. Millions every day, in fact.

Think about your last trip to the supermarket. What billboards did you notice along the road? Were any cars sign-written? What ads played on the radio?

When you arrived at the shops, what packaging did you see first? Did you notice any branding on the back of your receipt? Were any customers wearing company uniforms?

You get the picture. It's literally everywhere (and we haven't even mentioned smartphones yet!)

In order to be successful, we must find ways to rise above the noise and stand out from the crowd. How? Your POD (Point of Difference) - also known as your UVP (Unique Value Proposition).

Your next step in the process is to think about the feature that is valued most by your customers and distinguishes your brand from competitors'. What sets you apart from the rest? What makes your business unique? Here's a few ideas to get you thinking:

> Perhaps it's 20+ years of experience in your industry

> Maybe it's your eco-friendly products or practices

25

➤ It could be an innovation that others haven't implemented yet (e.g. a new app or software)

➤ Or a promise to your customers (e.g., "we're available to contact 7 days a week!")

Mini Task

Write down your POD.

Tip: If your POD is hiding in the depths of your business owner brain and you are struggling to locate it, why not ask some of your current clients directly?

It could be a simple phone call to say, "What made you choose us, Janet?"

You might be surprised at the answer!

Branding Basics

Today it is easier than ever to launch a business and promote it online. Competition, therefore, is tough! Creating a strong, recognisable brand that centres around your POD is just another way to stand out from the crowd. If you can do this properly, you're already streets ahead of the rest.

Let's take a look at what "the rest" are up to!

Mini Task

Take a few minutes to scroll through your Instagram or Facebook feed. Pick out 5 accounts at random and have a look at their overall profile.

At a glance, can you tell what kind of business it is? Do you get any personality-based vibes (i.e. do they look bright and bubbly, or professional with muted tones?) Are they using the same brand colours? These are just some of the things to think about when you are nurturing your own brand.

Consider some of the biggest brands in the world. I bet you can tell me in one second what McDonald's brand colours are? How about Coca Cola? Facebook?

Let's make it a little trickier and test your slogan knowledge.

Who knows what Nike's slogan is? Loreal? LG? McDonalds?

You get the point! It's all about mixing your brand colours with the imagery and content you want to be known for – the stuff that best represents your amazing business. Obviously, we are small businesses and will probably not become recognisable globally by our colours alone. But the aim is to become recognisable in your market – and not recognisable in general, but for YOUR specialty.

Don't have a slogan? Time to get brainstorming!

Don't have brand colours? Your logo is a great place to start. Consistency is key.

One final note on branding: it's not all about appearances. You must be 100% familiar with what you are selling, and most importantly you must believe in it. Only then can you expect others to believe in it, too.

Encouraging Engagement

It's easy to get caught up on social media "likes" - whatever the platform. But this is a mistake. Even if somebody has liked your post, this doesn't mean that they found it relevant, or even that they read the post at all. In the case of Instagram, they might have just liked the photo itself, double tapped and scrolled right past all that text you spent ages crafting (and on that note – sometimes less is more when it comes to text! More on this later).

The most valuable action a person can take on your post is to interact directly: commenting, clicking, saving or sharing. These are called "Engagement" metrics.

Social media platforms absolutely love it when people are actively engaging in your content, because it shows them that (A) – your content is valuable, and (B) – your content is encouraging people to use their platform for longer.

At the end of the day, that's all Facebook really wants - for people to spend more time using it!

So, how do we encourage people to engage with our posts?

We speak **with** our followers, not AT them. Here is an example:

(Speaking AT):

#TuesdayTip – to help you unwind after the chaos of work, take the time to write yourself a list for the next day.

Great tip, but is this likely to start a conversation on your page? Try instead something similar to the below:

(Speaking WITH):

#TuesdayTip – Being a small business owner is stressful! (Who can relate?)
We find that writing a "tomorrow" list helps our brains to unwind at the end of the day.
Do you have any other tactics that you've found useful? Share them below!

Or you can make the entire post about engagement:

We are looking for an amazing scheduling app for our social media! Please share your recommendations with us!

BOOM! People love to share their experiences and their comments will really boost the reach of your posts. Plus, you'll probably get some valuable tips out of it.

You'll find as you create engaging posts that you will build a community of sorts; each supporting each other with tips and suggestions. It might not be the same as meeting all your prospects in person, but it's a great way to encourage people to trust you before you ask them to purchase from you.

Did you notice how few words there were in that last example? It doesn't need to be much! Less is more sometimes, but it's all about balance.

Now that we've covered some quick ways to help your audience engage with you, let's go through a few tips on the longer posts; the storytelling.

The Art of Storytelling

Did you know that your readers are much more likely to engage and pay attention if you're telling a story? Transforming a "boring" educational post (however valuable the information) into your own tale will make the content real and relevant. Here is an example.

You are a bookkeeper. You want to explain to your audience the benefits of using Xero for their bookkeeping. Which one sounds better?

Example 1

When you switch to Xero for your bookkeeping, you can benefit from on-the-go account access, simplified payroll, and a range of various supporting apps to streamline your business operations.

Example 2

Johnny runs a small café in Canberra and is trying to choose a cloud-based software to manage his books. The café is thriving and he needs to make a decision quickly!

Johnny decides to sign up for a free Xero trial so he can check it out before committing (he's not very good with technology and needs to make sure it's user friendly!)

With Xero up and running, Johnny's staff check in to their shift using an app – that's payroll sorted! At the end of the day, the sales are synced to Xero already and Johnny can view his Profit & Loss from his phone whenever he needs to. Johnny clocks off at the end of the day knowing that everything is sorted for him.

Johnny is one happy camper!

Which one did you prefer?

For this example, we picked one of the most difficult services to market – on purpose. Being financial, it can be tricky to turn dry content to gold. But start to tell stories and people will listen! Especially café owners who want to be just like Johnny.

Audiences appreciate a personal connection with their speaker, and telling a story is a great way to not only establish credibility, but to connect with the people listening to you.

Be honest, and don't be afraid to share tales of your own failures or challenges. Stories are memorable. When people are able to relate, this is where the magic happens.

Think like your Customer

What better way to tell a winning story than by knowing your customer inside out? The good news is, we already drew up our customer personas earlier in the book.

But here's what lies at the heart of your biggest challenge: trust.

It takes time to build a relationship with your audience (especially online!), so remember that your marketing is a long-term commitment. Let your potential customers get to know you through valuable information posted on your blog, a responsive social media presence, and a consistent tone that is friendly and approachable, yet credible. It takes time, but it will be worth it.

When Less is More

It's estimated that visitors to your profiles decide within fifteen seconds whether to click away. That isn't a lot of time! Here's a few tips for keeping the shorter posts short:

➢ Use sub-headings to make it easier to scan through text

➢ Split up your content into short paragraphs

➢ Keep sentences short too - no longer than 15-20 words

➢ Use bullets to break information into lists (emojis can be a fun way to make bullet lists on social!)

Easy Instagram Photography

Imagine now that you own an IT business.

You might be thinking, there's only so many photos you can take of laptops and smartphones before it starts to get boring. And you'd be right.

The good news is, you can take a photo of almost anything and make it relevant to your world. Here are some examples of photos paired with caption snippets (some of these might apply to your business, too!)

➢ A photo of your coffee on the desk: "Basic Formatting Tips for Word" (because is there anything more frustrating than trying to neatly format a Word document? We think not!)

➢ A photo of your garden (or house plant) in bloom: "Integrating your software to work more efficiently is all about seeing GROWTH in your business."

➢ A photo from your last holiday: "Time is precious. Don't waste it getting frustrated with your laptop! Outsource those tasks you are not so passionate about and enjoy the extra time."

➢ A photo of your Halloween pumpkin: "IT is nothing to be afraid of!" Make use of holidays and trending events where appropriate (and of course, relevant)

➢ A photo of your car (especially if sign-written): "Did you know our services are completely mobile?"

➢ A photo of your team: Let us know who everyone is! What are their hobbies? What jobs do they do? (Avoid IT jargon, though!)

➢ A photo of your front door: "#MondayMotivation - If opportunity doesn't knock, build a door!"

31

Okay, so we probably got a little carried away with that last door example, but the point is that you can literally use any photo (within reason) and tell a story that relates back to the beauty of your business, whatever it may be.

This way, you won't be boring people with the same photos of computers or phones. This is especially important on Instagram, being such a visual feed!

Most phones today take spectacular photos and we always recommend posting your own photos rather than sourcing them elsewhere. However, if you are really tight for time, there are some amazing stock photography sites – some with free downloads available. Don't forget though, that other businesses might be using the same photos.

Tip: Make your own background props on a budget!

If you need a nice background to place your props, have a look in the shops for some book cover contact paper (preferably in your brand colours). Stick a decent size square to a piece of timber or corflute, and voila! You've got yourself a very inexpensive little studio prop. Perfect for taking your very own, uniquely branded photos.

Video Marketing

What's the best thing about video marketing? Just like all of the best things in life, it's completely free. All you need is a smartphone or camera – and some time to shoot.

Depending on your business, you might choose to post some helpful tips for clients, or show some "Behind the Scenes" footage of how your company operates.

Here's a fun example! With many women attempting to die their hair at home (especially during the COVID-19 lockdowns), hairdressers could create a short video series to demonstrate how to die hair at home (or better yet, how not to do it!)

Personal trainers might share some quick home workout videos, for example "Step by Step Squats" (does anybody really do those correctly?)

Dog groomers might show viewers how to clip their pet's nails, or the best way to brush their coat without the dog running away.

If you have an Instagram account for your business, posting your videos as "Stories" and saving them to a "Highlight Reel" is an effective way to showcase all your best video content; including tips, tricks, behind the scenes footage and company updates.

Tip: Don't be afraid to show your face on camera!

Although it might be daunting, customers are curious and love to see the personality behind your business operations!

Here's an example of what your highlight reels might look like:

This one is comprised of bookkeeping tips, behind the scenes content, inspirational quotes, customer reviews, end of financial year tips and marketing tips. These little reels in combination provide 3 key benefits:

➢ Educate the customer on areas they might be interested in

➢ Promote the business using testimonials

➢ Showcase the personality of the business using inspirational quotes and behind the scenes fun.

Mini Task

Brainstorm which highlight reels you want to showcase on your Instagram profile. You might create a reel dedicated to promoting other amazing local businesses, or you might have a "Products" or "Services" tab for followers to browse like a shop.

Step 4: Evaluate, Evaluate, Evaluate

"Every failure is a lesson. If you're not willing to fail, you're not ready to succeed."
Unknown

Social Media Metrics

Here we arrive at the "numbers" part of the social media equation. Hooray! For many of you, this might be the most exciting part of the book: the detective work.

There's a saying we love that goes: "Marketing without data is like cycling with your eyes closed".

(Do not try this at home!)

A lack of knowledge on what works for your business and what doesn't, puts you at serious risk of wasted time and money. There is no "one size fits all" approach; every business is unique and therefore deserves its own strategy. In addition, reviewing your insights and results on a regular basis is especially important today, because these numbers are never likely to stay the same.

Explaining how to track metrics is essentially a book in itself, so for now we're going to cover the most important ones for you to keep track of.

Understanding even just the basics, such as -

➤ What content works

➤ When it works

➢ How it works (what platforms)

➢ Who your audience is?

- will ensure your time, effort (and possibly money) spent on marketing is not lost. The legend below lists some of the metrics you should consider when reviewing your organic posts and ads. Have a look at each of these, then follow the step-by-step guide below.

Legend

Engagement: any measurable interactions with your social content such as shares, comments, likes, and clicks.

Engagement Rate: (likes + comments + shares + clicks + follows) / Impressions

Interactions: (Instagram) Likes, Comments, Saves, Story Replies

Facebook "Fans": the number of people who saw any of your posts at least once, usually grouped by age and gender.

Impressions: the number of times your posts have been seen, regardless of how many people saw them.

Organic Reach: Organic reach refers to the number of individual users who saw the posts that you posted for free (i.e. no paid advertising).

Reach: the number of individual users who were reached by your post (i.e. they saw it in their newsfeed or directly on the page).

Reactions: usually referred to as "Likes". Options on Facebook are "Like, Love, Haha, Wow, Sad, Angry". Options on LinkedIn are "Like, Celebrate, Love, Insightful or Curious".

Unique Visitors: users who visit your page at least once. Each visitor to the page is only counted once. If they access the page again, it still only counts as one visitor.

Metrics: Step by Step

Step One:

Look at the metrics in the list above for each of your platforms (you can find these in the **"Insights"** section of your business pages). Make sure the results are from the last 30 days, or however often you would like to be checking, e.g., you might choose to check fortnightly instead.

Step Two:

Don't just look at them, nod and move on to the next task. Write the results down, either in your notebook or in an Excel file. That way, each month you can make comparisons as to where you improved, and where there is now room for improvement.

Step Three:

Get creative with your thinking! Have a look at the best performing posts: can you see any patterns? Why do you think that post performed best? Was there a consistent time of day that was generating poor results?

Step Four:

From the conclusions you have made, write yourself a little to-do list for the next month of social media scheduling. For example, yours might look something like this:

> ➢ *Before & After posts are performing well, use this content at least once per week.*
>
> ➢ *Avoid Saturday morning posts!*
>
> ➢ *Call to Action "Find Out More" is generating more clicks than "Call Now".*

Sometimes you will look at your metrics and feel disheartened that your efforts haven't paid off. We have all been there, so please don't feel discouraged. You will make mistakes with your posts and ads, they are inevitable. But without them, we would never improve! It's what you do afterwards that counts.

Post didn't perform well? Have a look at your insights to see where you might have been lacking. Maybe you didn't target the right audience, or your "Call to Action" (e.g. Learn More or Call Now) was not clear enough.

You won't always get it right BUT you will learn some valuable stuff with every little setback.

NOTE: Do _not_ get caught up in followers!

A common concern for business owners is that their social media efforts are not producing any real results. But when we ask what is meant by "results", most often the answer is: "We have hardly any followers."

It is <u>so</u> important to remember that followers are only truly valuable if they are genuinely interested in your business. If you have 10k followers, but none of them purchase from you, would you consider that your efforts paid off?

If you have 100 followers that have been engaging with your content and clicking through to your website, you are on a much better path to conversion. So, if you take absolutely nothing else from this book, we want you to know **not to stress about followers.**

Our advice is to focus your efforts on growing organically and taking the time to really understand your audience. If you are using paid tactics, that's great too! But don't underestimate the importance of replying to comments, engaging with your followers, and creating posts that are valuable (not "salesy!")

Sure, it might seem like a lot of effort, but that's how relationships are built, right? Over time.

When your prospects are ready to switch, you will be top of mind.

If you get stuck with finding or analysing your social media metrics, please don't hesitate to reach out.

Reporting

One of our favourite ways to stay on top of our marketing results month-to-month is to create a report that highlights the key findings most relevant to your business.

For example, if you are only interested in finding out more about your Instagram audience, your report might look something like this:

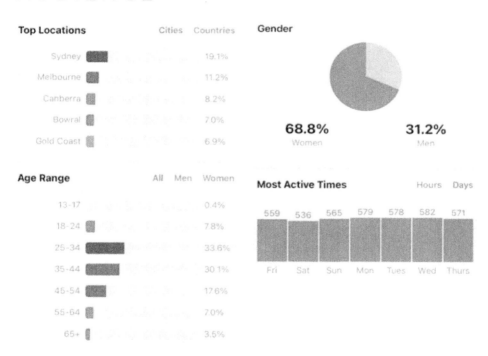

If you are more interested in the correct time of day to post on Facebook, you might see a graph that looks like this:

For more advanced tracking, you can look at your Google Analytics page to discover how many of your website visitors came from social media:

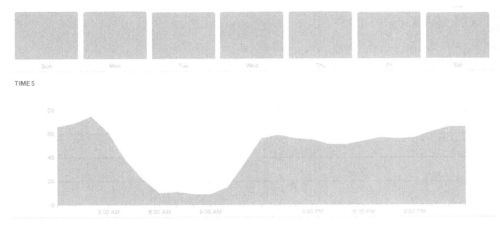

TIMES

Note: All of this data can be found from either your free Google Analytics account (if you don't have one, jump on now and get one!), or the Insights sections of your social media accounts.

Top Channels

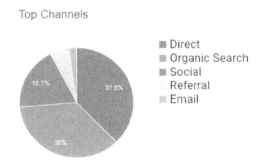

■ Direct
■ Organic Search
■ Social
  Referral
■ Email

Your report certainly does not need to be fancy. First and foremost, it should be practical. Whatever numbers or visuals will paint the patterns for you is what you should use. Some people love graphs, others prefer pie charts, line graphs or simple Excel spreadsheets. Google Analytics will even generate a custom report for you, if you are keen to save a little extra time.

Hint: A helpful little surprise is waiting for you at the end of this book …!

Find out what works best for you and make it your own.

Seeking Feedback

I'm sure you can tell by now that you need to do at least a little bit of research before taking off with your marketing. But the research doesn't need to stop at the beginning (and actually, it shouldn't!) We encourage you to be curious throughout your entire marketing journey; look at your analytics for numeric data, but also seek qualitative feedback from those around you.

Regardless of marketing, it is inevitable that your business will need to adapt to the shifting demands of your customers over time, especially as technology advances and those pesky customers are expecting more from us! The best way to avoid falling behind and becoming invisible as a result, is to stay "in the know" with what your customer wants at all times. This comes back to the "listening" concept we talked about earlier.

Take every opportunity to seek feedback from your customers, followers, colleagues and peers. Is this marketing effective? Would you buy this product if you saw my ad? What did you think of our latest post? Did you read it? (Open-ended questions are best if possible!)

Don't stray from criticisms but digest them as if they are brain food. Mistakes are how we learn, after all.

Note: Make sure your approach is not intrusive and try not to overwhelm people with too many questions! Everybody is busy and may not have the time or patience to offer detailed feedback (not regularly, at least). Split your questions up so your customers only need to answer one each. That way, they may spend more time on a valuable response.

Step 5: Above and Beyond

"A person who never made a mistake never tried anything new."
Albert Einstein

Blogging Basics

We know this is a book about social media. But it wouldn't feel right to leave out one of the best companions for your social media page: your blog!

If you know you have no time or patience for a blog at this stage, we won't be offended if you race ahead to the next chapter. But if you're interested, blogging is a low-cost, powerful channel of communication to reach existing customers and new leads.

The purpose of blogs is essentially to provide value to your readers (while helping to enhance your Search Engine Optimisation). SEO is a story for another day, but basically Google rewards business pages that are active and publish fresh content consistently! So there's another reason to create one. Plus, it may save you from having to answer numerous basic questions via email, as it can serve as a one-stop-shop for people searching for information.

Blogs are generally shorter than articles, making them easy to read, topical and sometimes light-hearted. You can use them to share business news (e.g., events, birthdays, milestones), advise people of any changes, promote upcoming sales or discounts, provide sneak previews, or even run contests.

One of the best benefits is that you can use your blog to encourage newsletter sign-ups, making it a golden lead generation tool. People that sign up are obviously interested in the content you're posting, so you know you're capturing the right audience!

Tip: If you are thinking of creating a blog, our advice is to start with the FAQs section of your website.

Break each blog down into a tip or FAQ that you can answer; preferably something that is related to your business AND that you are passionate about.

We've listed below several of our basic blogging rules, together with some snippets of The BookSitters blog page which is updated regularly with bookkeeping tips and industry updates.

Basic Blogging Rules

Put time aside to blog regularly if possible. The most successful blogs release new content at least once a week or fortnight, and they stick to a regular schedule. Not only are blogs a great way to tell your story, they also tell Google that your website is active and ready for business.

Blogs are part of the social media mix, so the same rules about storytelling and engagement apply. You want your content to be personal, engaging and memorable – not just promotion-based.

Lessons from three pricing stories

John's Story

Times were tough, so John decided he had to drop his prices below his competitors. The results seemed gratifying. Business picked up quickly and when John looked around his shop, he could see his sales staff were always busy with customers.

Then came the call from his accountant. "Aren't the sales figures great?" said John, getting his bit in first. 'Yes", said the accountant, "impressive sales indeed. That's

Sharing is caring! Cross-promote your blog content over various social media channels. If you've just posted a new blog entry, add the link to your Instagram bio, create a LinkedIn post or share the link on your Facebook page.

Our latest blog post is jam-packed with forecasting tips ᴖ ᴖ PLUS it includes a free downloadable forecasting tool.

Happy forecasting!

#Cashflow #BookkeepingTips

https://www.thebooksitters.com.au/a-beginners-guide-to.../

THEBOOKSITTERS.COM.AU

A Beginner's Guide to Cash Flow Forecasting - The BookSitters

Short and sweet is often key. Write "to the point" and make the text easy to scan with short sentences and subheadings.

On that point, try to use dot points. If the article is **"5 Marketing Tips"**, dot point the 5 tips so that they can be easily found (most people are guilty of quickly scrolling through the content to find out what the 5 tips are!)

5 Xero Mistakes Business Owners Make and How To Avoid Them

If you've just started working with Xero, it's normal to make a few mistakes while you're learning. We see mistakes that are quite common – and unfortunately costly – so you should be aware of them if you want to get the most out of Xero's powerful cloud accounting system.

1. Not connecting all the bank and credit card accounts dedicated for your business

Make sure that you keep all your business bank and credit card accounts synced to Xero to ensure that you don't miss any sales or expenses in your reports.

Make use of your keywords and include them in the text (use the ones you wrote down earlier but remember not to fall into the trap of "keyword stuffing").

Don't get carried away with the focus of your blog; choose only ONE topic to focus on. What is one piece of valuable advice you could share with your audience? It doesn't need to be very long (we all have short attention spans these days anyway); just enough to get your value across.

If you've already written content on the same topic, link these posts together. It will strengthen your blog because it shows Google that you are somewhat of an expert on the subject.

Contact your local bookkeeper

The information your bookkeeper or accountant can provide on your small business bookkeeping can go a long way to helping you make smarter decisions. Our team of friendly bookkeepers are passionate about supporting small businesses with all financial and accounting needs.

Whether you're just after some financial advice around benchmarking and cash flow monitoring, **bookkeeping tips**, basic bookkeeping services or assistance selecting an accounting package such as **MYOB**, **Xero**, **Quickbooks Online** or **Receipt Bank**, we are more than happy to help.

If your website allows, pop in some bright visuals in your brand colours to freshen up the page (especially if your blog covers a dry topic like bookkeeping!)

The Number 1 Thing You Need to Know About Your Business

20/12/2020

Improving cash flow: How to get paid faster

08/12/2020

Five Ways to Manage a Healthy Cash Flow

25/11/2020

Update your business plan for a new year

20/11/2020

Sponsored Ads

Is it worth the spend?

One of the best things about marketing on social media is that it's completely free, if you want it to be. Many businesses find success by posting organic content consistently and by engaging with their audience as we talked about earlier.

If you are in your earlier stages of business with a limited budget to spend, you might choose to start off with organic posts. If this is the case, you can read ahead to our 101 content ideas and start scheduling!

However, if you have a little budget to spare and want to give ads a crack, read on.

Our favourite thing about sponsored ads is that you don't need to spend much. We've heard stories of business owners spending as little as $2 per day. That's less than a coffee, for all you caffeine lovers!

Our second favourite thing about sponsored ads is the tangibility of your output. One of the most frustrating things you will find with marketing is that it can be difficult to tell if it's working or not.

If you were to run a newspaper ad for example, the newspaper will give you its readership numbers. But you have no idea if people are actively reading the ad, how many people are reading it, or if anybody has taken action on it.

It's the same story with radio ads. How do you really know how many people listened? Even if they heard your ad, were they really paying attention? Were they people in your target audience? Was it relevant to them at all?

Remember what we said earlier about being deaf to the advertising "noise"? This is one of the biggest challenges for us as marketers.

Of course, you won't know absolutely everything about how your sponsored ads performed. But you will be able to select the audience who sees it in the first place. You will find out how many people saw the ad and how many people clicked on it. If you post a video, you'll be able to see how many people watched 25%, 50% and how many watched the whole thing. The metrics available – even if they aren't 100% accurate – are there for you to use in improving your strategy if nothing else.

Although there are others, our recommended platform for sponsored ads is Facebook and this is the platform we will cover in this chapter.

Why Facebook?

Google how many Facebook users there are in the world.

There is your first answer. The opportunities to reach your audience are substantial! But here's a few other reasons why we love Facebook Ads:

➢ They aren't just for Facebook, in fact, you can choose to have your ads placed on Instagram as well. There is an option to select "Automatic Placements" and Facebook will determine where your ads are shown for the best results. Tick from us!

➢ We covered this before, but they're affordable! Since Facebook ads target your audience precisely, they can ensure a relatively low cost per click. Just set your budget and you'll be charged up to your maximum limit (e.g. if your budget for the month is \$100 but only \$80 is spent, you'll only be charged \$80).

➢ They are relatively easy to set up, in comparison to others like Google AdWords.

➢ The targeting abilities are simply amazing! You can micro target by selecting age, location, interests, job titles; you can even exclude people from seeing your ads (for example, you might not want that pesky other local financial advisor to see what offers you're promoting). This is exactly why we spent a whole chapter on defining your audience. If you've already got all that detail written down in your trusty marketing notebook, you will know exactly what to choose when it comes to creating sponsored ads (Facebook will suggest things for you, too!)

➢ You will have access to valuable data to monitor each ad, so you know if your ads are performing as they should or if you need to tweak your strategy.

➢ "Word of mouth" exists on social media, too! When someone interacts with your ad (likes, comments or shares) their friends may be notified. Those friends may visit and like your page as well, or click the link. People trust their friends and family much more than any advert and Facebook ads take full advantage of this.

➢ You will be able to choose your objective for each ad. For example, you might choose to drive traffic to your website. You might opt for more Facebook followers, or for more page engagement. You might want to encourage attendance at an upcoming event. You might simply be looking for greater levels of brand awareness in your local area. You could even be looking to generate leads. The options are endless and fun to explore!

➢ Facebook offers plenty of resources online to help you schedule effective campaigns and you can use these tools to walk you through the process. Stay tuned for Facebook offers as well, as they have been known to offer free phone call assistance to business owners looking to set up ad campaigns. It can be a little bit of trial and error in the beginning, but the best way to know is just to get started.

Tips for your first Facebook Ad

You might have heard the saying: "the best social media ads don't look or feel like ads at all". We couldn't agree more. The more you can make your ad look like something you might post on your personal feed (within reason, of course), the more likely it will be appealing.

Have you ever seen a sponsored ad as you were scrolling through your feed, and it annoyed you because it was completely irrelevant?

Or perhaps it was too relevant and you felt like your privacy had been invaded? Here's an example:

My partner and I had been at a party where the cocktails served were made from Mr Consistent mixers. The cocktails were yummy and we were talking about them the next day. It was a simple chat – no Google search, no visiting their social media profiles.

What ads did we see on our Instagram feeds the next day? Mr Consistent of course! He's certainly consistent if nothing else. And although we did enjoy those cocktails, we aren't big drinkers and certainly weren't looking to buy any mixers for ourselves.

The point is, choose your audience carefully. Don't waste your spend on the wrong people! Be sure your offering is something they're truly interested in and remember that social media is "social" media.

Once you've scheduled your ad, don't opt for the "set and forget" method. Especially in the first instance, you must keep an eye on the results. It might seem tedious but it truly will pay off. Once you discover your sweet spot in relation to the correct audience and content, you may simply maintain your efforts and reap the rewards of greater traffic to your website. Winning!

Facebook is an excellent advertising medium and we do recommend giving it a go. The key is to define your target audience carefully and ensure that the right people see your ads.

Since the Ads platform is consistently changing, we recommend searching for Facebook's educational material on creating ads, as they will provide step by step advice on the most up to date versions for desktop and mobile.

Please feel free to contact us at any time for assistance with Facebook Ads.

A Gift from Us to You: 101 Social Media Content Ideas

"Old ways won't open new doors."
Unknown

Congratulations, you've made it to the finish line!

By this point, your accounts should be set up and ready for scheduling some amazing content to make your business shine online. Brace yourselves! We're about to give you a smorgasbord of ideas for your small business.

(If you haven't got one already, now is the time to set yourself up with a scheduling tool.)

Below, we have listed 101 of our favourite content ideas to get you going on your social media journey. They are split into four categories or "bites":

TEACH your audience something new
ENTERTAIN your following
PROMOTE your products and services
BUILD a relationship with your audience.

Make sure to pick a selection of your favourite ideas from all four of the categories, rather than just one. The idea is to post a valuable blend that pairs education with some fun stuff, too.

51

Something to keep in mind as you choose your content: the people who need your services probably don't realise it yet. For this reason, **your posts need to sell the problem you solve, not the product or service itself.**

For example, imagine that you are a business selling thermos mugs. Instead of talking about the double wall options or the 10 different colours available, you should be describing the comfort of a warm, homemade drink while you're on the go. But this is just the beginning ...

> ➢ Talk about those cold mornings where your fingers are too frozen to move; the days you really need a handwarmer with you on the train.

> ➢ The mornings where you wait in line at the coffee shop for an hour and you end up being late for an important meeting.

> ➢ The day there was a new girl working at the cafe and she served you a burnt coffee.

> ➢ Tell us about the time your paper coffee cup was dodgy, and you spilt coffee all over your white blouse.

> ➢ Talk about the fact that you are lactose intolerant and only drink a rare form of coconut/soy/almond/cashew milk that the cafes don't stock.

> ➢ Or that you like 12 spoons of sugar with your tea and you're too embarrassed to order this in public.

There are so many different scenarios to choose from and each is solving a problem that one of your customers might face, instead of boasting about boring product benefits. All you need to do is pick one for each week!

Remember how we identified our POD (Point of Difference) earlier? Make sure you've got this written down on a post-it note in front of you as you schedule your content. Whichever of your favourites you pick from this list, it's important to weave your POD in there too, wherever possible (without sounding salesy).

Don't worry! We've provided lots of great examples to get the ideas flowing.

Mini Task

Write down some of your favourite bites from below, preferably a selection from each category.

Teach

Bite One: Sultana Muffin

Plain but rich in nutrients, these ideas should TEACH your audience something new.

1. Share the link to one of your latest blog posts.

2. Share a piece of industry news. For example, marketers often give the "heads up" when there are exciting new Instagram or Pinterest features.

3. Share a free resource. Have you developed any webinars, cheat sheets or checklists for your business?

4. Share ONE "Quick Tip" from your business (Example: Quick Hairstyling Tip).

5. Share tips from complementary businesses (Example: financial professionals might share a quick tip from Xero or MYOB).

6. Share a "How To" video (Example: How to Teach your Pup to Sit).

7. Answer a commonly asked question in your industry or an FAQ from your website. See a payroll example below:

   Q: Are employers required to pay staff over the holiday period?

   A: It depends on the individual business and the agreements in place – chat to us if you're unsure about your payroll over the Christmas period.

8. Share a "Step by Step" screenshot video (Example: see **@thebooksitters IGTV**)

9. Cover seasonal topics. For example, the end of financial year is a big content topic in the accounting world. Get started with your tips well ahead of time, because these seasonal events tend to creep up every year!

10. Share an interesting statistic (Example: If you're a dietician, you might write: Did you know McDonald's sells 75 burgers per second?)

11. Share other interesting tips that are not necessarily related to your business. It could be cooking, working remotely, gardening, or simply being a mum. Why not explain how you juggle working at home with regular clients, twin toddlers and the neighbour's cat that keeps wandering over to your place? Whatever the scenario, someone is sure to find it relevant (and entertaining if nothing else!)

12. MythBusters: bust a myth about your industry! Is it true that hairdressers spend 2 hours on their own hair each morning? We'd love to find out!

13. Don't be afraid to share posts from other accounts (as long as you tag and credit the author). Not only does this broaden the scope of the knowledge you share, but the other account is likely to be appreciative that you shared their post.

14. Share the contact details or websites of relevant bodies people might need to know about (for example, in the accounting world it might be the Taxation Office).

15. Tell us what a person in your line of business actually does. It seems obvious, but many people don't know what a bookkeeper does, for example. To avoid a very lengthy post, you might choose to split this up into a series of shorter posts.

16. Host an online course. Think of the obstacles your clients face and create a quick course or webinar to help them address that issue.

17. Teach people about your product or service. How much should they expect to pay for a hairdresser, for example? What features or materials should they be looking for in handmade jewellery? You might be surprised at how effectively this transparency will build trust with your audience.

18. Create an Instagram Reel for a step-by-step guide. For example, if you sell coffee beans, show us how to make an espresso martini!

19. Create mini quizzes on your story with topics surrounding your business. For example, if you're a gardener, you might ask "Which of these is NOT a spring-flowering bulb?" You'll find that people will take a guess even if they have no idea, simply because they're curious about what the answer is. Don't forget a "Call to Action" at the end (Example: Find out what flowers to plant this season on our latest blog post).

20. Did you Know: Surprise us with a random fun fact! Call it "Fun Fact Friday" or something that is quick and easy to consume. For example, as a lash and brow expert you might write: "Did you know the Mona Lisa has no eyebrows?" Throw in a photo of the Mona Lisa to keep your audience engaged (Likelihood that they will zoom in on her face? 100%). Engagement = boosted!

21. Share some knowledge that can be applied in a broad sense to several business types. For example, if you are a HR specialist, you could create a post that answers: "What kind of information should I share with my staff?" Don't assume this is common-sense stuff, because it's not always the case.

22. Segment your knowledge for different groups. Not only will this showcase your amazing expertise in different subject areas, it will also allow you to reach a greater audience. For example, as a hairdresser you might run a separate post for each hair colour e.g. "Conditioning tips for brunettes/Maintenance tips for blondes". Wherever possible, extend the usage of your posts with smaller snippets. You will end up with so much more content to take advantage of!

23. Share your best working from home or working remotely tips (if applicable). In today's world, working from home is something many of us have had to trial – some of us with more success than others. Did you have a routine that worked well for you, or an app that was super helpful at keeping you on track? Share!

24. Is there an "audit" or "health check" you can guide your followers through? Examples below:

> **Marketing Service**: Website Health Check (Do the links on your website work, is it easy to read, is it easy to book, etc.)

> **Hairdresser**: Hair Health Check (Do you have split ends, is it looking flat, are your products free of parabens, etc.)

> **Bookkeeper**: Cash Flow Health Check (Calculate your cash flow for the upcoming month, how is it looking?)

> **Groomer**: Pet Coat Health Check (Is it falling out in clumps around the house? Are your products free of nasty chemicals?)

> **Mechanic**: Windscreen Wiper Health Check (Are your wipers making an audible noise when in use? Do they leave any marks?)

Okay, so we might be getting a little carried away here! But have a think about what kind of "health check" or audit you could offer your prospects from a distance; something that is simple to follow in steps and potentially, something that may lead them to call you if all is not in order.

25. Most importantly, teach your audience about why it is that they need your product or service. Don't just sell them the benefits but go through those thermos mug scenarios for your own business and get your following educated on how you can improve their lives.

Entertain

<u>Bite Two: Vanilla Cupcake</u>

Fun and light, this content is not to be taken too seriously! Quick, easy and delightful to digest.

1. Behind the Scenes Snippets (Resist the urge to stage this; be authentic!)

2. Share some of your favourite quotes. Who doesn't love a little inspiration on their newsfeed?

3. "A day in the life of a ..." builder, personal trainer, dog walker?

4. Share a photo of your office space: "where the magic happens!"

5. Share a fun photo of your team in a Zoom meeting

6. Flashback Friday or Throwback Thursday. Tell us a fun fact about how your business has evolved over time. Share a photo of the sign-written car you had 15 years ago when you first started. Or the first business cards you ever bought. This stuff is SUPER interesting, and all comes back to the storytelling effect.

7. Make use of holidays and special events. For example, on Valentine's Day you might write: "Tell us one thing you LOVE about being a small business owner?" (this is a great one for encouraging engagement on your posts).

8. If you have any upcoming business events (e.g. Conferences, Roadshows, Staff Parties), try your best to take photos. Show everyone the fun team

behind your business operations - at the end of the day, people connect with people!

9. Share random days of the calendar (Examples: World Compliment Day, Pancake Day). If you run a Google search on this, you'll probably be able to find something for every single day of the calendar year.

   NOTE: Only pick those that are relevant and appropriate. Wine Week or World Sleep Day might not be the best to promote if you are supposed to be housekeeping or looking after people's finances, for example.

10. Feel Good Friday: Share something funny that happened to you today, or a fun fact about your pets (Example: we took our sheepdog to meet some sheep yesterday and she ran the other way!) The sky really is the limit when it comes to social media.

11. Fun Fact: Share some completely random knowledge that is not necessarily related to your business. People love to learn new things! For example, did you know humans are the only animals that blush?

12. Jokes. Who doesn't love a classic "Knock Knock"? For extra suspense, add some blank space between the statement and the punchline.

13. Share a photo of something that made you smile today. Maybe it was a new blooming flower in your garden, or the coffee from your local café was particularly scrumptious this morning. Show us your world; share the happy little moments!

14. Tell us your business story: when you started, what made you take the leap, what challenges you faced, what wins you celebrated and what encouraged you along the way. Other business owners will be inspired by your journey! You can split this up across several posts, for example, one might focus on the day you chose your logo and how you made that decision (Tip – start with the "About" content you wrote earlier).

15. Share any exciting updates and business developments, however simple they may be! Did you just receive a fresh box of business cards? Take a video and share it to your story. There's nothing more exciting than receiving something in the mail, right? (except for bills, of course)

16. Have you been on holiday recently? Show us your photos! Tell us where you stayed, what you ate, what you did, what you can recommend. Tag any restaurants or suppliers that stood out (they will be super grateful!)

17. Introduce any new team members. A video post would be most engaging and personal, but if that's a little too daunting, a simple professional photo and some info about their background would do.

18. Video content. Again, the sky is the limit. Remember though that people are busy, they don't have time to watch long videos and likely won't stay engaged for an extended period. Keep your videos short and sweet (no more than 3 minutes – unless it's going on IGTV) and use a subtitle tool to add your captions.

19. Share a GIF on a Friday! All you need to do is type "Friday" into the search bar and you're sure to find something amusing.

20. Share your favourite quotes pertaining to your specific industry. For example, a dentist might write: "Be true to your teeth, or they will be false to you."

21. Post imagery of the things you enjoy. We recently saw a great example where somebody had shared an image of a gorgeous office nook to inspire others to create a warm and welcoming workspace. Don't forget to credit the author.

22. Share some little anecdotes about your life. Remember, people love to read stories! Tell us about where you used to work, some of your old boss's craziest quirks; tell us about what you learned about that workplace and what you miss about it.

23. Memes: find some for your industry and share them! Who doesn't love a good meme?

24. Share photos or videos of your pets at work! We know it sounds silly, but we've actually tested this and found a significant rise in engagement with the use of dogs or cats in particular. Your dog isn't a good poser? No worries! Take a video of the struggle. The followers will love it.

25. Make the experience with your product or service interactive! For example, real estate agents are creating home video tours and 3D exploration tools. We have also seen some incredible examples with bath bombs where the videographer uses their hands to emphasise the texture of the product.

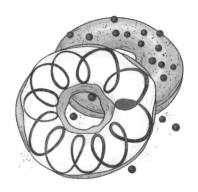

Promote

Bite Three: Iced Donut

Plump, fun & brightly coloured, this mouth-watering content is designed to attract and tempt.

1. Testimonials are GOLD when it comes to promotion because you are not boasting about your own business, somebody else is doing it for you. Ask for them and share them wherever possible! Marketing costs money, but word-of-mouth is free.

2. Take advantage of industry events and share content from other sources to boost promotion of your services. Global Bookkeeping Week is a great example in the financial world.

3. Share a case study from one of your clients: how you helped them to grow their business in 12 months, or how you crafted their dream garden in time for their daughter's wedding.

4. Tell us one unique thing about your service (Example: Did you know we offer a free trial period?)

5. Offer a special discount going into a new week.

6. Let people know that you offer free phone appointments (or whatever your special offer/POD might be).

7. Share your achievements. For example, if you've just become a Xero Gold Partner or finished your Masters in Architectural Design, be proud of your achievements and shout them from the rooftops. You might be surprised at how wonderfully supportive your new following is.

8. Share your business slogan. If you don't have one, start brainstorming! Think about your POD. As a real estate agent, you might pick something like "en route to your dream home" because you always go the extra mile. If you're a spray tan artist, you could be "the falcon team" because of your speed. Always be careful that you're not accidentally making negative connotations around your services. Take the spray tan example: speed might not create an attractive tan!

9. Sometimes you might choose to keep it simple with a short call to action: "Unsure about your cashflow situation? Give us a call. We're here to help". And that's all you need to say. It can be incredibly reassuring to see that businesses are offering free advice, especially during times of stress. Make sure that your contact details are clear and up to date on your profiles.

10. Share a quote related to your business; a subtle way to promote that your services are AMAZING and that every small business owner needs you. One of our favourites: "Behind every good business is a great bookkeeper."

11. Try cross-selling! Cross-selling is simply inviting your customers to buy a secondary item that naturally bundles with a product they're already purchasing. For example, if your customer is buying a dog lead, it might make sense to offer a collar, or even some poo bags to go with the purchase (you'll get optimal results when a complementary item is offered at a much lower price point).

12. Simple business announcements. We don't have time to call each of our clients with every single update (e.g. new staff, new hours), but social media is a good way to stay "in touch" without sacrificing too much time. That being said, when you do communicate with your customers via phone, email or in person, it's a good idea to encourage them to follow you on your social media platforms.

13. Run a contest. Offering a prize is a fantastic way to generate buzz online and in your community. You could work together with other local businesses in your area to extend your reach, with each company donating a prize to the basket.

14. Referrals. A referral program encourages customers to send their friends to your site and earn rewards for their efforts. It's a great way to generate low-cost advertising! Before long, you can have an army of loyal customers actively promoting your business. With every new referral, you exponentially increase the chance of getting more customers.

15. Remember how we talked about Karen's objections earlier? You can use social media to address the barriers that hinder your audience from purchasing. For example, if you're a swim instructor and you know that many of your customers are mums worrying about their kids getting sunburnt, tell them about the 5L bottle of sunscreen you keep by the pool at all times! Write down all the objections you can think of and create a post for each one.

16. Joint advertising. Good examples build on complementary industries. For instance, if you run a home aquarium cleaning service, you could work with a local pet shop. Together, you could offer a discount on your cleaning services, provided the customer buys their equipment (and fish) from the associated pet shop. Both businesses benefit!

17. Create a loyalty program. It is more expensive to acquire a new customer than to keep an existing one. For this reason, it is important that you strive to build a relationship with your customers. A loyalty program is a great way to do this.

18. Take advantage of national/international sale periods. For example, Black Friday is a great opportunity because you can offer an irresistible deal for only a short amount of time. Be sure to promote this for at least a week beforehand so your followers have time to browse your offering; they'll probably be looking at a lot of other goodies at the same time!

19. Provide something valuable for free (anything in numbers is a good idea!) For example, if you're a copywriter, you might create a post on "9 strong standout words to use for the best ad copy."

20. Tell us about your pricing or packages. This will depend on your business type, your competition and how transparent you'd like to be around your prices. For high involvement purchases that take a lot of consideration to make a decision (e.g. deciding on a builder), this might not be a possibility.

    But when it comes to low-involvement purchases (for example, buying a new hairbrush or candle), having to send a message to find out the price of every individual product can be frustrating, so make yourself a price list, or feature your shop on your feed. If your products are highly priced in the market, explain why. Be transparent! Are you using all locally-sourced materials? Is your product handmade? Your audience will respect you for your honesty around pricing.

21. Create a sense of reality around your product or service. For example, if you sell homewares, share a photo of the product in a real living space as opposed to it being featured alone. Explain how you would style the room with the product, what colours you would use, etc. If yours is a makeup service for example, explain how to create the look and what garments you would pair with it?

22. Create a carousel of product images (or a carousel of tiles listing your services). Try to make it pop with bright, on-brand colours and avoid using too much text on the images; sometimes the best way to promote is with eye catching imagery.

23. If your product needs a complementing product, be sure to promote the business or brand you recommend. For example, if you sell printers, chances are your buyers will need ink too (if you don't already sell it!) Don't leave them guessing.

    Another example is hairstylists - don't forget your followers will probably want their makeup done as well, so if you don't offer this service, let them know who you recommend. This is a perfect opportunity to create strategic alliances in your community where you support each other with recommendations.

24. Before and After. Who doesn't love these! Whether it's a renovation, haircut, garden makeover or an artist's workshop, these work an absolute treat. Another option is to post several photos of the journey itself (this works particularly well with builders and if you have the opportunity, time lapse and drone footage is an amazing way to feature your work, too).

25. Post a shoutout for your clients. We saw a great example recently of a window cleaner who'd posted photos of their work at a luxury resort. Rather than rattling on about what cleaning products they used, they took the opportunity to write about how amazing the views from the resort are. Photos were still posted with the gorgeous clean windows in sight, so it was promotional in a subtle way.

Build

<u>Bite Four: Croissant</u>

Simple but tasty, each new layer of content is designed to leave you wanting more. Warning: this dessert contains a few more layers than promised ...

1. First and foremost: Introduce yourself! What are your passions? What are your interests and hobbies? Your favourite food? Where did you grow up? Don't forget to include something to encourage conversation, for example: "I'd love to hear who you are and where you are from?"

2. Meet the Team. This is a great way to build trust and relationships from a distance. The value of putting a face to a name – especially in today's Zoom-driven world – is priceless. Tell us about everyone's roles in the office, but also tell us a fun fact about each of your team members.

3. Client Shoutout. Showcase a client's business! To explain why we do this, we'll use one of our all-time favourite marketing quotes: "Marketing is like a first date. If you only talk about yourself, there won't be a second one." So true! It is super important to tell your following about yourself, but sharing the success and brilliance of other businesses too is a credit to your caring and supportive nature.

4. Other Shoutout. Talk about a café, restaurant etc. you visited recently and what was great about it. Don't forget to tag them where possible (This

relates to positive experiences only! DO NOT use your business page to make negative comments about other businesses).

5. Why not share the link to your Google Review page? Here's a simple example:

    If you love the services we're providing, or the content we're sharing, we'd love it if you could take 2 minutes to leave us a review via the link below. Thank you so much for supporting our small business!

6. Personal Posts. You don't have to do this very often, but sometimes it might be nice to share something about yourself or your family. Share a photo of your office puppy and tell a story about something naughty she did. Tell us about the funny thing your daughter said to you this morning as she was hopping off to school. Remember, your audience might be a group of mums who can relate to the sassy teenage comment! It's all about building trust and allowing your audience to know you.

7. Share your business values. This tells clients how you run your business and how your staff are trained. Example values might be: <u>Professionalism, Care, Laughter</u>. These three simple words paint a fantastic picture about the type of service people can expect from you.

8. Show a photo of your team in uniform if applicable, and ask others, do they have a company uniform? What colour is it? (it's all coming back to engagement!)

9. Create a very simple engagement post, e.g. Happy Friday! What are your plans for the weekend?

10. Share a simple little "pick-me-up" – for example, "May your coffee be strong and your Monday productive" with a photo of your morning beverage. Easy as! Perfect for those times you don't have time to write a long spiel.

11. Share your involvement in community events and charity initiatives. For example, you might be participating in a "Relay for Life" event in which case, use your socials to rally support! Don't be afraid to share the links to your donation page. Giving back will raise your community profile and

provide free advertising, while creating goodwill as you help an individual or organization in need.

Schools, libraries, hospitals and not-for-profits all benefit from volunteers and community fundraisers. And if that isn't reason enough, customers want to support businesses that care.

12. Some of our favourite posts are those that express their support for small business. It can be as simple as listing the ways to support your local businesses. Examples: like a post, share a post, leave a nice review, comment something nice. All of which are $0!

13. Send out well wishes during holiday periods and make sure to let people know if your office is closing. Example: "Happy Easter from the team! Our office will be closed from Friday 2nd to Monday 5th, wishing you an egg-cellent Easter break."

14. Share a photo of your local area; the main street, a cute corner café or the duck park (especially if you live somewhere beautiful and scenic!) Locals in particular love this type of post - they might even share it.

15. Looking for a restaurant or café for a special occasion? Skip the Google search and ask your audience! Again, you are encouraging engagement and starting a conversation around the support of your local businesses. Plus, you're likely to find a real gem for your special event.

16. Create some video content and don't be afraid to show your face! Make a little "hello" video so others can get to know who you are.

17. Ask your following directly, what bugs them most about (insert your industry)? What do they most want to know about? What content would be most valuable to them? As the saying goes, "Don't ask, don't get." One of the best marketing strategies in our opinion, is the true and authentic demonstration of care.

18. Ask your following to share a GIF or emoji that best describes their week. This is a really fun and light-hearted activity that will encourage engagement while creating smiles. Do this on a Friday or midweek Wednesday.

19. Ask your following something simple and random. Example: Are you a coffee or a tea drinker? Comment with an emoji! Which team are you on?

20. As above, but centre around something that relates to your business. For example, an accountant might write "Share the GIF or emoji that best describes you at tax time".

21. Thank your following for supporting you and for interacting with you. People love to feel appreciated.

22. Share one of your favourite recipes, no matter your business type! Because let's be honest, who can scroll past a summer cocktail or winter warmer?

23. "Caption This". Just for fun, share a photo of something that stands out in a newsfeed, write "caption this" and enjoy the responses! Another great one for engagement.

24. What better way to build a community than to hire them? If you are looking to expand your team, why not use your socials to let people know about it.

25. Share your birthday with your following! Let us know how you will be celebrating, where you will go. What are some of your most valuable life lessons learned to date?

26. With so much of our lives and businesses in the cloud, if you come across an amazing app that makes your life easier, share it with us (especially if it's a free one!) In today's digital world, customers rely on the experiences of others so as not to be overwhelmed with the amount of choice available online. Sharing is caring.

27. Create a post on the days that are important to you and share why that is the case. For example, many business owners create posts for International Women's Day, along with a little note on celebrating women's achievements. Don't forget to use the hashtag (if applicable) to the event as it will improve your discoverability.

28. Share real customer stories via user-generated content. For example, if your business sells gift boxes, ask the recipient to take photos of the

surprised receiver. This is perfect content because it is real, raw, authentic, genuine and your followers will notice. Repost and tell your audience why they received the box and how excited they were (why not throw in a testimonial with it, too?)

Little Extras

"Don't let the fear of losing be greater than the excitement of winning."
Robert Kiyosaki

Frequently Asked Questions

When should I be posting on social media?

It depends on your own account insights. You can search this question on Google and it will give you some standard times/days to post but you are much better off looking at your own insights to see when your particular followers are online.

Back at the beginning of the book, you defined your audience. A tradie for example, is likely to be looking at their phone at a different time to somebody working late shifts in hospitality. The more you can personalise everything to your own audience, the better your marketing will perform for you. Remember, we're talking to **our** audience, not everybody!

What do I do if someone has left a nasty comment?

Unfortunately, it happens – whether you were in the wrong or not. But stay calm and don't let it upset you. As much as you might like to, don't delete the comment because it may provoke the troublemaker to keep spamming your account. Instead, reply with something short and professional, for example:

We are sorry to hear you feel this way (name). Please feel free to reach out to our friendly team on 04 (number) – we'd love to assist and provide a resolution where we can.

They are likely to reply to this but do not respond again - once is enough. Do not argue. Do not explain the situation in writing. All you are doing is showing other readers how courteous and professional you are. Short and sharp is key!

What is an organic post?

An organic post is anything you have posted for free (i.e. not "boosted" posts or sponsored social media ads). Many people rely predominantly on organic posts to grow their business. Although it is more time-consuming, it is a great option if you have a limited marketing budget at your disposal.

What is the difference between an ad and a post?

Where a post is generally organic (as explained above), an ad has had money spent on it. Ads are usually directed to a specific audience, and they will appear on newsfeeds as determined by the demographics you select. Once you see a sponsored ad on your feed, it might be difficult to locate it again because it exists on the newsfeeds of the advertiser's chosen audience, not necessarily on their page.

Should I invest in social media ads?

This depends on your marketing budget, your business type, and the objective you want to achieve. For example, if you're a business selling earrings, you've got a little bit of budget to spare and you want to drive traffic to the "Sale" section of your website, sponsored ads might be a great option for you, especially if you have carefully selected your target audience (as we did earlier). Sponsored ads tend to work especially well for products-based business where graphics of your product grab visual attention.

For services businesses, it can be a little more tricky. For example, if you're an advisor it can be difficult to find a tangible, pretty-looking object to showcase in an ad. With a smaller marketing budget, your spend may be better invested in local advertising or organic tactics, such as word-of-mouth and referrals.

We strongly advise seeking the opinion of a marketing professional on this. Every business deserves its own marketing plan and yours is no different. Your marketing expert will be able to advise on the best use of spend, platform and strategy for your unique business.

What NOT to Do

Incorrect Contact Details. Are the contact details on your profiles correct? Are there any broken links? Can customers call you by clicking? We know this sounds obvious, but it goes unmissed more often than you think and it will turn customers away in a heartbeat.

Talking in Jargon. If you do this on social media, people will assume you're the same in real life. For example, if you're a marketer, don't go on a tangent about pixels or SEO. People don't like to feel silly! Describe things in plain English; assume you are explaining everything for the first time to someone who has no idea (because most likely, they don't!)

Complicate your website. Think about the last time you visited a business website. How quickly could you find the page or answer you were looking for? Chances are, if you didn't find it pretty darn quickly, you would have been out of there in no time. Remember how we talked about being "deaf" to the advertising noise? The consequence of this is that our attention spans are SUPER short. We know we'll find what we want elsewhere, so why stick around trying to rifle through a million paragraphs trying to find it? Nobody's got time for that.

That being said, don't keyword stuff your website. Keep it clean and simple to navigate. You might think it's eye-catching and effective to go crazy with colours and patterns or moving bits and loud music (does anyone else hate this?) Simple is the best way.

Ignoring comments. In our engagement chapter, we talked about building trust by developing conversations and communities. Conversations are two sided! Don't expect everyone to rush and leave comments if you are not prepared to respond. If you are responsive and friendly, customers will see your interactions and know that you're reliable. It's just another building block for the Jenga of trust! You only need to turn your notification settings on and have a quick check each day.

Buying followers. Don't do it. Followers don't mean much if they are never going to engage in your services. Focus on building your own unique database of prospects.

Copy and paste. By all means, recycle your content. Just don't "copy and paste" (with the exception of hashtags). You should be able to change some words here and there to make it different on each occasion. People won't stick around if you're stuck on repeat.

Set and Forget. We're all for scheduling posts ahead of time, but we don't mean for you to schedule 12 months' worth of repeated posts, then never look at the account for the rest of the year. It is a process that does take time. Spend a moment – even if it's just once a month – looking at your stats; what's working, what's not. Respond to comments, engage, be present and show that your business is active and ready for new customers.

Automated messages. There's nothing worse than receiving a message with the wrong first name on it, or a message that is irrelevant to you, or a message that is simply spammy. If you have the time to reach out to people and personalise the message each time, go for it! Otherwise, most people these days will be able to tell if it's automated and they will be put off by the lack of personalisation (yep, we've all got bigger expectations as technology evolves!)

An example of a nice, personalised message might be:

Hi Stephanie, thanks for following us. Your feed is lovely — how long have you been running your candle business? Look forward to being part of your journey.

Stop interrupting what people are interested in. BE what people are interested in. Don't just post for the sake of posting, make sure what you're posting is valuable (if not, it's a waste of your time!) Ask yourself, if I was a restaurant owner / mum of 3 / first home buyer — would I find this useful or entertaining? A social network can provide quick updates on topics of interest, but that purpose is defeated if you post about trivial matters throughout the day.

Carelessness. Have you considered the possibility that your message might offend someone? Think about who has access to your profile. If there's any doubt whether your post is appropriate or acceptable, it's better to be safe than sorry.

Don't forget to spellcheck! We are not just speaking to creative writers, proof-readers, copywriters, and marketers. Spellcheck is for everyone! Yes, it can seem like a terrible waste of time. But take the time to read. Check for silly typos. Get someone else to check; sometimes an extra pair of eyes will spot things that you missed.

If you're a professional service making errors left right and centre, you won't look like a professional service! It's all in the detail.

A Parting Note

If you have made it to the end of this book with a clear idea of your audience, social media accounts optimised to showcase your business, and a plan to schedule some fresh content, you should be extremely proud of the work you have put in. This is no easy task if you're not a creative person!

We hope this book has provided you with plenty of fruitful ideas, inspiration, and valuable knowledge on promoting your own business using social media.

The next step? **Get started!**

One thing we will note is this: building a social media presence does take time and patience. It is not as simple as posting and waiting for the leads to come flooding in. But with a bit of thoughtful content creation, you will create a community over time. Remember, your following might not need a real estate agent, financial planner, builder or dog walker at the moment, but you'll be top of mind when that need arises.

We will leave you with a little personal anecdote of ours.

Last year we discovered that, despite the memes about house plants, it turns out that looking after your plant isn't too difficult - as long as you pick one that is low maintenance. We were gifted a Monstera Deliciosa (or "Swiss Cheese") plant just over 12 months ago, and the thing is still growing like crazy. We will soon need to barricade the kitchen door to stop it venturing into the fridge!

One might assume that we are pouring our heart and soul into this plant; talking to it each day, feeding, watering it and loving it to death. But in fact, this plant doesn't need much at all - just consistent water, and sometimes a little sunshine.

Digital marketing is much the same. Some weeks it might seem like your creative efforts are not returning great results. But marketing your business is a gradual process and does take time (at least 6 months!) to really make an impact.

Don't be disheartened if the growth seems a little slow at times. Keep up the consistent "nurturing" of your brand and you will notice a difference. When you are passionate about your business (and it shows!) your customers and prospects will be too. So, what are you waiting for?

Bonus

"Marketing is enthusiasm transferred to the customer."
Gregory Ciotti

We would like to take this opportunity to thank you for reading our book. In doing so, you have shown fantastic support for a small Australian business and we are truly grateful.

To show our gratitude, we invite you to download our BONUS item free of charge: <u>Monthly Marketing Report Template.</u>

To access your copy, navigate to the following web address:

<u>www.thebooksitters.com.au/your-bonus-gift</u>

You can customise this template to your own business needs, brand guidelines and personal style. We encourage you to track your social media results each month, using the template as your guide to a well-informed, profitable social media strategy.

If you have any questions, you may contact us at any time using the email address above.

Did you enjoy this book? Let us know! If you have a couple of minutes spare to leave us a quick review, we would be especially grateful for the support.

To your Marketing Success!

- The Sitters Team.

Printed in Great Britain
by Amazon